QUESTIONING HISTORY

THE LOUISIANA PURCHASE

Asking Tough Questions

by Nel Yomtov

Consultant
Tim Solie
Adjunct Professor of History
Minnesota State University, Mankato
Mankato, Minnesota

CAPSTONE PRESS
a capstone imprint

Capstone Captivate is published by Capstone Press, an imprint of Capstone.
1710 Roe Crest Drive
North Mankato, Minnesota 56003
www.capstonepub.com

Library of Congress Cataloging-in-Publication Data is available on the Library of Congress website.
ISBN: 978-1-4966-8468-4 (library binding)
ISBN: 978-1-4966-8814-9 (paperback)
ISBN: 978-1-4966-8488-2 (eBook PDF)

Summary: What was the Louisiana Purchase? How did it change the United States? How did it affect the future of the country and its people? These questions and others are examined to inspire critical thinking for young readers.

Editorial Credits
Editor: Aaron Sautter; Designer: Sara Radka; Media Researcher: Eric Gohl; Production Specialist: Spencer Rosio

Image Credits
Alamy: Classic Image, 28, Niday Picture Library, 14, Old Paper Studios, 32; Bridgeman Images: National Geographic Image Collection/Silverfish Press, 24; Getty Images: Bettmann, 11, 39 (bottom), Ed Vebell, 19, Kean Collection, 23, Stringer/MPI, 39 (top); Granger: 9 (top), 12, 21; iStockphoto: tonda, 5; Library of Congress: 16; New York Public Library: 15; Newscom: Picture History, cover (back), 34; North Wind Picture Archives: 6, 13, 20, 26, 31; Pixabay: MIH83, background (throughout); Shutterstock: chrupka, 7, 27, 35, 40, Everett Historical, 18 (top left, top right), Monkey Business Images, cover (front), Peter Kunasz, 44–45, Sean Pavone, 43; Wikimedia: Public Domain, 9 (bottom), 10, 37, 40–41 (top)

Table of Contents

Was the Louisiana Purchase Worth the Price? 4

CHAPTER 1
How Did the Louisiana Purchase Happen?....................8

CHAPTER 2
What Did People Think of the
Louisiana Purchase? 14

CHAPTER 3
Did the Louisiana Purchase Keep Its Promises?........22

CHAPTER 4
How Did the Louisiana Purchase
Affect Native Nations?...................................30

CHAPTER 5
What Is the Legacy of the Louisiana Purchase?.......38

More Questions about the Louisiana Purchase........ 44

Glossary..46
Read More..47
Internet Sites...47
Index...48

Words in **bold** are in the glossary.

Was the Louisiana Purchase Worth the Price?

Historians have called the Louisiana Purchase the greatest real estate deal in history. In 1803 the United States bought the Louisiana Territory from France for $15 million. The lands included 828,000 square miles (2.1 million square kilometers) and nearly doubled the size of the United States. The country was suddenly one of the largest in the world.

FACT
The Louisiana Purchase included more land than Spain, France, Italy, Portugal, Holland, Switzerland, and the British Isles combined.

The Louisiana Purchase stretched west across the Great Plains from the Mississippi River to the Rocky Mountains.

The Louisiana Purchase also helped the United States to become one of the world's richest countries. The land was filled with valuable minerals and farmlands. It featured important waterways, large forests, and wildlife. Before long, a huge wave of settlers would begin moving west to build a new life.

WHAT WAS THE UNITED STATES LIKE IN 1800?

In the early 1800s, the United States was made up of 21 states and territories. The country only included land between the Atlantic Ocean and the Mississippi River.

At that time most U.S. citizens were farmers. They grew wheat, oats, and corn, and raised livestock. Rice, tobacco, and cotton were the chief crops grown in the South. American industries, such as shipbuilding and textiles, were in the early stages of development.

Most people lived and worked as farmers at the time of the Louisiana Purchase.

At first the Louisiana Purchase seemed to be a good deal. The new lands would allow for growth in farming, industry, and trade. But was it a good deal for everyone? How would it impact the lives of Native nations who already lived in the territory? How would it impact the lives of enslaved people? Would it allow slavery to expand in the United States? Follow along to take a close look at the Louisiana Purchase and consider if it was really worth the price.

U.S. Farm Production, Early 1800s

■ Dairy, cattle, hay

■ Corn, wheat

■ Cotton

■ Rice

■ Tobacco

CHAPTER 1

How Did the Louisiana Purchase Happen?

WHY DID PRESIDENT JEFFERSON WANT TO BUY LOUISIANA?

The Louisiana Territory stretched northwest from New Orleans, Louisiana, to the Great Plains. In 1800 France signed a **treaty** with Spain to gain the lands in the territory. By this time, France was a powerful European empire. And its ruler, Napoleon Bonaparte, wanted to expand France's power in the world.

U.S. President Thomas Jefferson and other officials were nervous about France owning the land. Jefferson believed the Mississippi River and New Orleans were needed for shipping U.S. goods. He also wanted America to expand westward. The Louisiana Territory could help grow the country's size and wealth. But if France owned the land, Napoleon could block these goals. Jefferson believed France's presence was a threat to America's security.

The port at New Orleans, Louisiana, was important for shipping and trading furs, farm crops, and other U.S. goods to other countries.

President Thomas Jefferson

WHY DID NAPOLEON WANT TO SELL THE LOUISIANA TERRITORY?

Napoleon wanted to expand France's power in North America. But he faced several problems. First, he needed money. War with France's long-time enemy, Great Britain, was looming. Second, France had recently suffered a great defeat. The country had failed to put down a **rebellion** in its colony in Haiti.

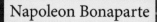
Napoleon Bonaparte

In the Haitian Revolution (1791–1804), enslaved black people successfully fought for their freedom and the end of French rule on Haiti.

Napoleon realized that keeping the Louisiana Territory could lead to conflict with the United States. He feared that America would try to seize New Orleans by force. Napoleon couldn't risk war with Great Britain and the United States at the same time. Instead, he chose to **negotiate** to sell the land. Doing so helped avoid conflict with one country while providing money for war efforts against the other.

HOW WAS THE LOUISIANA PURCHASE FINALLY SETTLED?

President Jefferson didn't realize that Napoleon needed money. He was concerned about the Spain–France deal. Could he still make a deal with Napoleon to use the Mississippi River and New Orleans? For Jefferson, the best solution was to simply buy New Orleans from France.

Robert Livingston (center) and James Monroe (right) signed the Louisiana Purchase Treaty on April 30, 1803.

In September 1801 President Jefferson turned to Robert Livingston, the U.S. Minister to France. He told Livingston to make a deal to buy New Orleans and western Florida from France. Jefferson later sent James Monroe to help. Monroe was a former Minister to France. Many months passed but no deal was struck.

After some time, Napoleon realized that he'd likely lose Louisiana in an armed conflict. So he offered to sell the entire territory to the United States. Livingston and Monroe jumped at the offer. They signed the Louisiana Purchase Treaty in 1803. The deal was almost done.

The Louisiana Territory, 1803

U.S. officials didn't know the exact borders of the Louisiana Territory. The treaty stated the lands included "Louisiana with the same extent that it now has in the hand of Spain . . ." U.S. officials believed the deal also included West Florida. But it didn't. Those lands belonged to Spain.

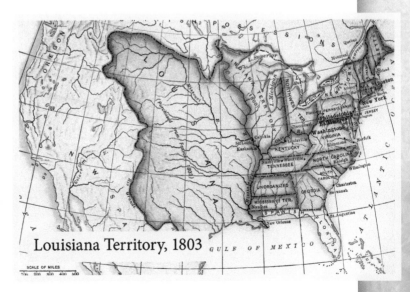

Louisiana Territory, 1803

CHAPTER 2

What Did People Think of the Louisiana Purchase?

DID SOME PEOPLE OPPOSE THE DEAL?

On December 20, 1803, the U.S. flag was raised in New Orleans. The ceremony showed the official transfer of the Louisiana Territory to the United States.

Napoleon Bonaparte approved the treaty on May 22, 1803. But the U.S. Congress still had to approve it. What did U.S. citizens think about gaining the new land? One newspaper, the *National Intelligencer*, reported that there would be "widespread joy of millions" at the historic event.

But that wasn't true of everyone. Many claimed that the land was too large and would be impossible to manage. Others felt that America couldn't afford it. Former Representative Fisher Ames wrote, "We are to give money of which we have too little for land of which we already have too much."

Fisher Ames

Money wasn't the only issue. Some people thought a deal with France would anger Great Britain. America had only recently fought the Revolutionary War (1775–1783). Many people wanted to avoid another costly conflict with England.

FACT
The United States didn't have $15 million to buy the Louisiana Territory. The government had to borrow the money from British banks and pay it back with **interest**. When the loan was repaid in 1823, the total cost was more than $23 million.

The U.S. Capitol was much smaller in 1803 than it is today. There were a total of 176 representatives and senators that year.

DID THE DEAL THREATEN TO DIVIDE THE NATION?

Many U.S. citizens feared that the Louisiana Purchase would weaken their states. They claimed that settlers would create new states and send representatives to Congress. This would reduce the eastern states' political power. Some easterners even threatened to **secede** from the union if that happened.

Opponents of slavery also opposed the deal. They feared that slavery would expand across the new land. They thought the number of slave states would grow larger. This would increase friction between northern and southern states over the slavery issue.

Members of Congress had many heated debates about the deal. Finally, the U.S. Senate approved the Louisiana Purchase Treaty on October 20, 1803.

Was the Deal Legal?

Opponents of the purchase claimed that President Jefferson didn't have the power to add new land to the United States. However, the U.S. Constitution grants the president the power to make treaties with foreign governments. Since the Louisiana Purchase was part of a treaty, Jefferson argued that his actions were legal.

Meriwether Lewis

William Clark

WHO EXPLORED THE NEW TERRITORY?

President Jefferson wanted to learn more about the Mississippi River and the lands west of it. He had read the reports of Robert La Salle. The French explorer had traveled through the region in 1682. "It is nearly all so beautiful and fertile," wrote La Salle. "There can be no doubt that colonies planted here would become very prosperous."

Jefferson was eager to find out more about the Louisiana Territory. He asked Congress to fund an **expedition** to explore the new lands. He chose Meriwether Lewis, his personal secretary and a captain in the U.S. Army, to lead the expedition. Lewis chose William Clark, an army lieutenant, to join him as his co-commander. In May 1804 the 45-man crew, called the Corps of Discovery, set out from St. Charles, Missouri, to **survey** the territory.

The expedition began their journey up the Missouri River in May 1804.

Traveling on the rivers was difficult. The crew often had to carry their boats around rough river rapids and waterfalls.

The Corps of Discovery spent the next 28 months exploring the lands of the Louisiana Purchase. They traveled 8,000 miles (12,875 kilometers) from Missouri to the Pacific Ocean and back. The party first traveled up the Missouri River by **keelboat** and dugout boats. As they traveled, they took detailed notes about the climate, soil, animals, plants, and people they encountered.

In October 1805, the explorers reached the Columbia River and began traveling west. A group of Shoshone people led the Corps across the rugged mountains in Montana. In mid-November, the Corps finally reached the Pacific Ocean. Lewis and Clark returned home with a wealth of knowledge. They brought back accurate maps, animal and plant samples, and **artifacts** from various Native nations.

FACT

In November 1805, Lewis and Clark met Sacagawea. She was an English-speaking member of the Shoshone people. For more than a year, the 17-year-old woman helped guide the party and served as a translator. Without her help, the expedition's mission may not have succeeded.

CHAPTER 3

Did the Louisiana Purchase Keep Its Promises?

WHAT PROMISES DID THE LOUISIANA PURCHASE MAKE?

The Louisiana Purchase Treaty promised, ". . . the inhabitants of the **ceded** territory shall be incorporated in the Union of the United States." These people were to have ". . . the enjoyment of all these rights, advantages, and **immunities** of citizens of the United States." This meant that the people living there would have the same rights as all U.S. citizens.

By 1850 New Orleans had become one of the busiest and most important cities in the United States.

In the following years, the Louisiana Purchase brought great growth for the U.S. economy. Farmers and fur trappers spread across North America all the way to the Pacific Ocean. The country soon became a world power. But did everyone share the benefits provided by the deal? Would the treaty live up to its promise of guaranteeing "the enjoyment of all these rights" to all people?

Thomas Jefferson owned more than 600 enslaved people during his life. Many of them lived and worked at his Monticello plantation in Virginia.

HOW DID PRESIDENT JEFFERSON VIEW SLAVERY?

Thomas Jefferson wrote in the Declaration of Independence that ". . . all men are created equal." He often wrote about the evils of slavery, and thought it should be stopped. He called it a "hideous blot" that threatened the survival of the nation.

However, Jefferson was a farmer and owned many enslaved people himself. He didn't object to the spread of slavery in the Louisiana Territory. He failed to support plans to outlaw slavery in the new lands. Jefferson remained silent on the issue. Some experts believe his loyalty to large planters was greater than his desire to stop slavery.

The Louisiana Purchase had set the stage for a major future conflict. The arguments over slavery would eventually rip apart the country and lead to the Civil War (1861–1865).

After the Louisiana Purchase, tens of thousands of black people were bought and sold into slavery in New Orleans.

DID THE LOUISIANA PURCHASE LEAD TO MORE SLAVERY?

The Louisiana Purchase Treaty promised that people in the new lands would have rights like any U.S. citizen. But supporters of slavery demanded that the practice should be allowed to expand. Lawmakers in Congress battled over the issue. Eventually slavery was legalized in Arkansas, Louisiana, and Missouri. By 1860 there were more than 550,000 enslaved black people in those states.

New Orleans became a major center of the slave trade. In the years before the Civil War, nearly one million enslaved black people passed through the city. They were sold to white land owners across the South. The Louisiana Purchase helped many white slaveowners to become wealthy. For the thousands of black people who were forced into slavery, the new lands became a place of suffering and misery.

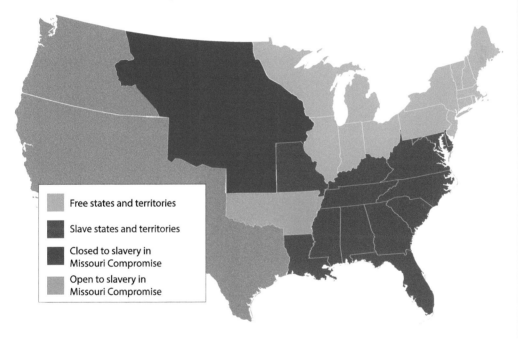

Free states and territories

Slave states and territories

Closed to slavery in Missouri Compromise

Open to slavery in Missouri Compromise

The Missouri Compromise

In 1820 Congress passed a law admitting Missouri to the Union as a slave state. The law admitted Maine as a free state. The Missouri Compromise of 1820 kept the number of slave and free states equal. The Compromise legalized slavery in Missouri. But it banned slavery in other lands north of present-day Arkansas.

WHAT WAS "BLEEDING KANSAS"?

The issue of slavery continued to cause problems for many years. In 1854 Congress passed the Kansas-Nebraska Act. This law allowed the citizens of those states to decide if slavery would be legal, rather than the U.S. government. The Act **repealed** the Missouri Compromise of 1820, which would have outlawed slavery in both territories.

In the 1850s, opponents of slavery in Kansas were known as Free-Staters. Supporters of slavery were often called Border Ruffians. The two sides often clashed violently over slavery and whether Kansas would be a slave or free state.

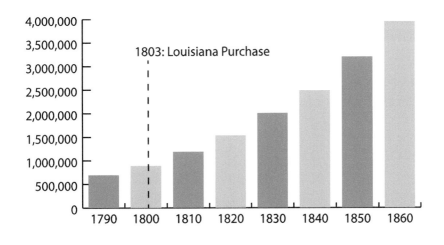

Proslavery and antislavery settlers poured into Kansas to vote on the issue. Violence soon erupted between the two sides. Between 1854 and 1861, as many as 200 people were killed in the fighting. The conflict became known as "Bleeding Kansas." It was just one example of the anger between the free and slave states, which eventually led to the Civil War.

CHAPTER 4

How Did the Louisiana Purchase Affect Native Nations?

HOW DID THE U.S. GOVERNMENT TREAT NATIVE PEOPLE?

In 1803 about 600,000 Native people lived in the United States. They owned and governed their own lands. Several Native nations lived on lands in the Southeastern states. These included people from the Cherokee, Choctaw, and Chickasaw nations. It also included the Seminole people and groups from the Creek Confederation.

President Jefferson believed America's strength and wealth should come from farmers. Large-scale farming needs a lot of land. The government desired the Natives' lands in the Southeast to boost U.S. farming. After the Louisiana Purchase, the government took several steps to force Native nations off their land.

In the early 1800s the Seminole people made their home in the marshes and wetlands of the Florida Everglades.

Seminole leader Osceola refused to sign a treaty to give up his people's lands. He stabbed the treaty with his knife instead. Osceola later led his people against U.S. forces in the Second Seminole War.

The government bought some land from Native nations. But they were paid less than the land was worth. U.S. officials also convinced some Native people to trade their land for new lands further west. The government then sold the Natives' lands to white farmers at a higher cost to make a profit.

FACT
President Jefferson supported forced removal of Native people from their southeastern homelands. "Our strength and their weakness is now so visible that they must see we have only to shut our hand to crush them," he wrote.

Some Native nations in the Southeast did not trade their lands with the government. But many white settlers soon flooded into those areas anyway. They wanted the Natives' lands for themselves. So they pressured the U.S. government to acquire them. But the government needed a reason to act.

In the 1830s tens of thousands of American Indian people were forced to leave their homes. Thousands died on the "Trail of Tears" during the journey to Indian Territory west of the Mississippi River.

WHAT WAS THE INDIAN REMOVAL ACT?

From 1814 to 1818, General Andrew Jackson battled Native nations in the Southeast. One conflict was in response to a Creek attack on an army fort in Alabama. Jackson's troops defeated the Creek. They were forced to give up their lands in Georgia and Alabama.

In another conflict, Jackson's forces destroyed Seminole settlements in Florida. The U.S. government accused the Seminoles of protecting runaway enslaved black people. White slaveowners demanded that they be captured and returned. The Native people were defeated and forced off their land. The enslaved people were sent back.

By 1830 Andrew Jackson had been elected president. That spring Congress strongly debated the Indian Removal Act. Many people opposed it. They thought it was immoral and illegal. But the Act narrowly passed, and President Jackson signed it into law.

The Act gave the government the power to force Native nations to give up their lands. They would be given lands in the Louisiana Purchase in exchange. Native people who refused to trade their land were forcibly removed. Most were sent to Oklahoma. During the journey west, thousands of them died from starvation, disease, and extreme temperatures. The brutal 1,000-mile (1,600-kilometer) forced march became known as the "Trail of Tears."

Native Nations Lands and
Trail of Tears Routes, 1830

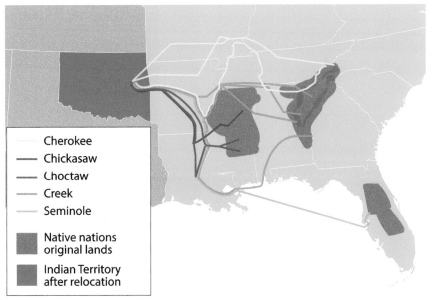

Cherokee
Chickasaw
Choctaw
Creek
Seminole

Native nations
original lands

Indian Territory
after relocation

WHAT WERE THE PLAINS WARS?

In later years large conflicts took place between Native nations and U.S. forces on the Great Plains. From the 1850s to 1890, bloody battles were fought from Texas to Montana. Much of the conflict resulted from the U.S. government breaking its treaties with Native people. White settlers kept pushing farther west into Native lands, and the government failed to pay what it had promised.

In 1862 the Dakota people in southern Minnesota were starving. The U.S. government was busy fighting the Civil War at that time. Much of its resources went to support the war effort. As a result, the government failed to send food and resources to Native people that had been promised in various treaties. The Dakota nation grew angry and began attacking several white settlements. Hundreds of people on both sides were killed during the Dakota War of 1862.

In 1890 U.S. troops murdered as many as 300 Lakota people in the Wounded Knee Massacre in South Dakota. Could these violent conflicts have been avoided if white people hadn't spread west after the Louisiana Purchase?

In the end, most Native nations couldn't stop the flood of white settlers. Many Native people had to move off their lands and onto reservations. But these were often located on poor land in remote locations. Native people couldn't continue their customs or live as freely as they had before.

FACT

The Native nations had one major victory in 1876. Led by Crazy Horse and Sitting Bull, thousands of Native warriors battled U.S. forces at the Battle of the Little Big Horn in Montana. Also known as Custer's Last Stand, 263 U.S. soldiers were killed in the battle, including Lieutenant Colonel George Armstrong Custer.

What Is the Legacy of the Louisiana Purchase?

WHAT WAS "MANIFEST DESTINY?"

As the United States spread farther west, many people supported the idea of "manifest destiny." They believed the country would one day own land from the Atlantic to the Pacific Ocean. By 1850 this belief had become true. The United States controlled all the lands between the East and West coasts. Settlers eagerly answered the call to fulfill America's "destiny." Hundreds of thousands of settlers poured into the West. They came from across the United States and nearly every country in the world.

Settlers headed west on the Oregon Trail, the Mormon Trail, the Santa Fe Trail, and other routes. Some wanted to strike it rich looking for gold or silver. But most came to start a new life. They claimed Native lands to grow crops and raise livestock. The new farms produced food to feed the growing nation.

The Oregon Trail crossed the much of the lands of the Louisiana Purchase. In the 1800s, hundreds of thousands of people journeyed on the trail to start new lives in the West.

The Homestead Act of 1862

In May 1862, President Abraham Lincoln signed the Homestead Act. This law allowed settlers to buy 160 acres (65 hectares) of land for a small fee. Roughly 1.6 million land claims were granted in 30 states. Most of the claimed land was part of the Louisiana Purchase. But the Homestead Act had a downside. To make way for the settlers, thousands of Native people were pushed off their land. They were forced to live on reservations.

Along with new lands, rivers were just as important for the country's growth. The Mississippi River, Missouri River, and others were important waterways. They enabled U.S. goods to reach domestic and international markets. River travel allowed trappers and traders to grow rich from the fur trade. It also let merchants bring in goods to sell to the settlers who were traveling west.

Transcontinental Railroad
Built 1863–1869

Promontory Summit, Utah

Sacramento, California

San Francisco, California

Omaha, Nebraska

— Central Pacific

— Union Pacific

— Added later

FACT

In 1869 the First Transcontinental Railroad was completed at Promontory Summit, Utah. The 1,776-mile (2,858-km) railroad stretched from Omaha, Nebraska, to San Francisco, California. Suddenly, making the long journey across the United States was cut from several months to less than a week.

Over time, transportation was improved on rivers, new roads, and railroads. This contributed to the growth of stronger farming and manufacturing industries. Thanks to the Louisiana Purchase, the United States became one of the wealthiest countries in the world.

WHAT WAS THE TRUE COST OF THE LOUISIANA PURCHASE?

The Louisiana Purchase was an incredible opportunity for the United States. For a modest amount of money, the country gained great riches. The territory's valuable resources helped the United States to become a major world power.

Yet not all Americans benefitted from the greatest real estate deal in history. Millions of black people were sold into slavery. White slaveowners considered black people to be less than human and forced them to work for no pay. Many suffered severe beatings or worse.

The expansion of slavery also caused conflict between white people who either supported it or opposed it. Those conflicts eventually tore the country apart and led to the Civil War.

The Gateway Arch in St. Louis, Missouri, is a huge monument to westward exploration and expansion of the United States. It is sometimes called "The Gateway to the West."

Meanwhile, many Native nations lost their homelands. They lost their traditions and cultures. Thousands of Native people lost their lives as they were forced to move west.

For a few cents an acre, the United States doubled its size and grew rich and powerful. But the deal caused misery for many people. Was the Louisiana Purchase really worth the price? You'll have to decide.

More Questions about the Louisiana Purchase

How did the United States get the money to pay for the Louisiana Purchase?

Napoleon required the U.S. government to borrow the money from British banks. The British unknowingly provided Napoleon the money he needed to wage war on them.

What is the Louisiana Purchase worth today?

In 1803 the United States bought the Louisiana Purchase for about 4 cents per acre. Today land costs between $1,000 and $4,000 per acre. Today, the value of the Louisiana Purchase is about $1.2 trillion.

What did Lewis and Clark learn on their expedition?

Lewis and Clark gathered a lot of information about the Louisiana Territory. They discovered waterways, mountain ranges, and even a route to the Pacific Ocean. Without their work, developing the new territory would have been much slower and more difficult.

How would the United States be different without the Louisiana Purchase?

Without the additional resources gained in the Louisiana Purchase, the United States may not have grown as large and wealthy as it is. What might have happened if France had not sold the territory to the United States? What would the country look like today?

GLOSSARY

artifact (AR-tuh-fakt)—an object, such as a tool or weapon, used in the past that was made by people

cede (SEED)—to give up property or power as part of a treaty or pact

expedition (ek-spuh-DI-shuhn)—a long journey made for a specific purpose or goal, such as exploring or searching for something

immunities (i-MYOON-i-tees)—legal protections from something, such as being unfairly accused or punished for a crime

interest (IN-tur-ist)—a fee paid for borrowing money

keelboat (KEEL-bote)—a large, flat river boat used for carrying freight

negotiate (ni-GOH-shee-ate)—to reach an agreement or make a bargain through discussion and compromise

rebellion (ri-BEL-yuhn)—an armed fight against a government

repeal (ri-PEEL)—to officially cancel something, such as a law

secede (si-SEED)—to formally withdraw from a group or organization

survey (SUR-vay)—to measure land in order to make a map or a plan for how to use it

treaty (TREE-tee)—an official agreement between two or more groups or countries

READ MORE

Harris, Duchess, and Kate Conley. *The Indian Removal Act and the Trail of Tears.* Minneapolis: Abdo Publishing, 2020.

Herschbach, Elisabeth. *Slavery and the Missouri Compromise.* New York: AV2 by Weigl, 2020.

Lawrence, Blythe. *The Louisiana Purchase.* New York: AV2 by Weigl, 2020.

Shea, Therese M. *The Louisiana Purchase and the Lewis and Clark Expedition.* New York: Britannica Education Publishing, 2018.

INTERNET SITES

Louisiana Purchase Facts for Kids
kids.kiddle.co/Louisiana_Purchase

Manifest Destiny Facts for Kids
kids.kiddle.co/Manifest_Destiny

Westward Expansion: Louisiana Purchase
www.ducksters.com/history/westward_expansion/louisiana_purchase.php

INDEX

"Bleeding Kansas", 28–29

Bonaparte, Napoleon, 8, 10–11, 12–13, 14, 44

Civil War, 25, 27, 29, 36, 42

farming, 6, 7, 23, 25, 30, 41

France, 4, 8, 10, 12–13, 15, 45

Great Britain, 10, 11, 15

Great Plains, 8, 36

industry, 6, 7, 41

Jackson, Andrew, 34–35

Jefferson, Thomas, 8, 12–13, 17, 18–19, 25, 30, 33

Kansas-Nebraska Act, 28

La Salle, Robert, 18

Lewis and Clark expedition, 19–21, 45

   Sacagawea, 21

Louisiana Purchase

   cost of, 4, 15

   economic growth from, 7, 23, 27, 40–41, 42, 43, 45

   location of, 8

   reactions to, 14–17

   resources of, 5, 42, 45

   settlers of, 5

   size of, 4

   value of, 44

Louisiana Purchase Treaty, 13, 14, 17, 22, 26

Louisiana Territory, 4, 8, 11, 13, 15, 19, 25

"manifest destiny", 38

Mississippi River, 6, 8, 12, 18, 40

Missouri Compromise of 1820, 27, 28

Native nations, 7, 21, 30, 32–33, 34–35

   conflicts with, 34, 36–37

      Battle of the Little Big Horn, 37

      Dakota War of 1862, 36

      Wounded Knee Massacre, 36

   loss of lands, 32–33, 34, 35, 37, 39, 43

      Indian Removal Act, 34–35

      "Trail of Tears", 35

New Orleans, 8, 11, 12, 13, 27

Pacific Ocean, 20, 21, 23, 38, 45

Revolutionary War, 15

slavery, 7, 17, 25, 26–27, 28–29, 34, 42

Transcontinental Railroad, 41

U.S. Congress, 14, 16–17, 19, 35

U.S. population, 7

westward expansion, 5, 8, 36, 38, 40

   Homestead Act of 1862, 39

   Oregon Trail, 38